PERSEPHONE

GODDESS OF SPRING AND
QUEEN OF THE UNDERWORLD

BY   MONTE   PLAISANCE

Thessaly Publications

Houma, Louisiana

Persephone

Goddess of Spring and Queen of the Underworld

BY MONTE PLAISANCE

© 2023 Thessaly Publications

ISBN: 9798326012494

INTRODUCTION

Persephone, weaving thoughts, veils minds in blissful haze,
No other crafts this art, when death's shroud holds its embrace.
To shadowed realms, they tread, where the departed dwell,
Through gates in solemn black, where souls in silence swell.
Despite their fervent pleas, the barrier stands firm,
In death's abode they linger, yearning souls in term. ~ Monte Plaisance

In the ancient city of Larissa, there lived a young woman named Callista, whose heart knew the gentle whispers of love but had not yet danced the sacred vows of marriage. Fate, however, had a different plan for her, and on a fateful day, she met an untimely end.

As Callista descended into the underworld, she found herself in the shadowy realm of the dead. An eerie silence hung in the air, and the black gates loomed ahead. Fear gripped her soul as she approached, but to her surprise, the gates swung open with an otherworldly grace.

Beyond the threshold, she entered a place bathed in a dim, ethereal glow. A figure emerged, clothed in regal grace and adorned with a crown of darkness. It was Persephone, the Queen of the Underworld, who extended a welcoming hand to Callista.

"Fear not, child of the mortal realm," Persephone spoke with a voice that echoed through the caverns. "You come to the realm of shadows, a place between worlds. Here, love and union take different forms."

Persephone guided Callista through the serene fields of asphodel, where shades of the departed wandered in quiet contemplation. The goddess shared tales of love and loss, of mortals who found solace even in the afterlife.

"Your journey here is not a punishment but a transition," Persephone reassured Callista. "In this realm, the essence of love endures, transcending the boundaries of mortal vows. Embrace the beauty that lies within this realm of shadows."

Callista, comforted by the words of Persephone, discovered a sense of peace in the underworld. She learned that love was not bound by the constraints of earthly unions but flowed through the ethereal currents that connected all souls.

As the seasons shifted in the world above, Callista found solace in the company of the shades and the wisdom of Persephone. In the embrace of the underworld, she discovered a love that surpassed the confines of mortal life, a love that whispered through the eternal echoes of the shadows.

Ancestor Altar with Chythroi Pots

PERSEPHONE'S SACRED STORIES

UNDERSTANDING THE DIFFERENT TYPES OF MYTHS

Myths can be categorized into five distinct types, each serving a unique purpose in conveying meaning and understanding the divine world. Let's explore these categories to gain a deeper insight into the world of myths:

1. THEOLOGICAL MYTHS:

    - Theological myths delve into the essence of the gods and their divine nature.

    - They do not employ physical forms but rather contemplate the very core of the gods' existence.

    - An example of a theological myth is the story of Kronos swallowing his children, which symbolically expresses the essence of the divine through allegory.

2. PHYSICAL MYTHS:

    - Physical myths are those that depict the activities of the gods in the physical world.

    - For instance, interpreting Kronos as Time, we can view the divisions of time as his "children" who are metaphorically "swallowed" by Time, their father.

PSYCHIC MYTHS:

- Psychic myths focus on the activities of the human soul.

- They highlight how thoughts, though originating within the soul, can eventually extend beyond the individual and onto external objects.

- An example would be viewing Kronos as the preserver of his divine children, who are expressions of his own divine soul.

3. MATERIAL MYTHS:

- Material myths are often embraced by the less educated.

- These myths stem from ignorance and involve attributing divine status to material objects, such as naming the earth Gaia or equating moisture with Zeus.

- It's important to note that while certain objects, herbs, stones, and animals may be considered sacred to the gods, asserting that they are the actual gods is erroneous. They are more like symbolic representations, akin to calling both the sun and its rays "the sun" in common language.

In conclusion, these five types of myths offer different perspectives on the divine, allowing us to explore and understand the mystical world in various ways. They serve as a bridge between the realms of the gods and human comprehension, enriching our understanding of the divine and the profound meanings hidden within these ancient tales.

PERSEPHONE AND MINTHE

In the underworld, there lived in the river Cocytus, a river nymph named Minthe. Minthe, a nymph of vibrant allure. Enveloped by the embrace of the god Hades, she reveled in her beauty, unaware of the impending twist of fate. For Minthe's existence took a drastic turn when the dark lord Hades, was seized by the pains of love for Persephone, and took her to be his bride.

Minthe, inspired by an envious flame, let her heart be consumed by folly. In her misguided jealousy, she raved loudly, boasting that her superior form and unparalleled beauty were greater than Persephone's and daring to claim that Hades would cast his new bride aside and return to her in time. Such arrogant words reached the ears of the goddess Persephone and sparked a flame of wrath within her.

Infuriated by Minthe's audacity, Demeter descended upon the nymph with a tempest of anger. With each step, the earth trembled beneath her feet, and in her fury, she trampled Mint with relentless force. The nymph's arrogant boasts were silenced, and the once proud beauty succumbed to the vengeful might of the goddess.

As Minthe lay shattered beneath the feet of Persephone, the goddess was overcome with regret for her rash actions and wept. When her divine tears mixed with the remains of the broken nymph, a fragile herb sprouted. This herb now bears the name Mint, after the fallen nymph, and is a testament to the consequences of arrogance and the wrath of the divine.

COMMENTARY: *The myth of Minthe serves as a compelling narrative that transcends time, conveying a profound moral lesson about the perils of arrogance and the consequences of* *challenging divine authority. At its core, the story unfolds as a cautionary tale, warning against the destructive nature of envy and the havoc it can wreak on both mortal and immortal alike.*

Minthe, once a nymph of vibrant allure, becomes a tragic figure consumed by jealousy. Her ill-fated decision to boast of her beauty and predict the downfall of Persephone reflects the dangers of unchecked pride and the folly of underestimating the powers beyond mortal comprehension. The myth underscores the fragility of mortal desires when pitted against the divine order.

The divine retribution meted out by Persephone exemplifies the wrath that befalls those who defy the natural order. The relentless force with which Minthe is trampled serves as a stark reminder that arrogance, especially when directed against the gods, invites swift and severe consequences. The myth thus imparts a moral lesson about humility, urging individuals to recognize their place in the grand scheme of the cosmos and refrain from challenging the balance ordained by higher powers.

The unexpected twist in the story, where Persephone's remorse leads to the emergence of the Mint herb, introduces an element of redemption. The Mint herb, named after the fallen nymph, becomes a symbol of transformation and renewal. It signifies that even in the face of divine retribution, there is room for growth and the possibility of redemption through remorse and reflection.

In Thessalian religion, mint holds significance in funerary rituals, alongside rosemary and myrtle. In ancient times Mint also played a crucial part in the preparation of the kykeon, a fermented barley beverage integral to the Eleusinian Mysteries. These mysteries, offering hope for the afterlife to initiates, incorporated mint as an essential element.

PERSEPHONE AND THE KORONIDES

In the ancient land of Aonia, a dire plague gripped the city of Thebes in a relentless embrace, claiming the lives of many. Desperate for relief, the elders of the city dispatched officers to consult the oracle of Apollo at Gortyne, seeking guidance from the divine.

The god's response echoed through the sacred chambers, declaring that to quell the wrath of the gods of the underworld, two willing maidens must be offered as sacrifices to Persephone and Hades. A daunting task it seemed, for none in the city dared to embrace such a fate.

Yet, fate unfolded in mysterious ways. A humble servant-woman, touched by a sense of duty and compassion, brought the oracle's decree to the daughters of Orion, the two Koronides. These maidens, immersed in their loom's intricate dance, listened to the plea for sacrifice. Unwavering in their devotion to their fellow citizens, the sisters, without hesitation, accepted the burden of death upon their shoulders.

With solemn determination, the Koronides cried out to the gods of the underworld, their voices resonating through the still air. Thrice they proclaimed their willingness to be sacrificed, and with resolute hands, they thrust their perónisi (pins that hold their garments in place) into their own shoulders, gashing open their throats in a sacrificial ritual.

As their lifeblood stained the earth, the benevolent gaze of Persephone and Hades fell upon the maidens. Touched by the purity of their sacrifice, the gods chose to spare them from the depths of the underworld. Instead, the bodies of the Koronides vanished, replaced by a celestial transformation.

Upwards they ascended, borne by unseen forces, until they graced the night sky as radiant comets. Mortals, witnessing this celestial marvel, named the heavenly bodies after the maidens who willingly embraced death for the salvation of their city. The two Koronides, once earthly maidens, now adorned the heavens, a testament to the selfless sacrifice that transcended mortal boundaries and earned them a place among the stars.

COMMENTARY: *The myth of the Koronides and their selfless sacrifice to quell a devastating plague in Thebes carries profound symbolism and offers insight into the complexities of human nature, mortality, and the interplay between life and death. This ancient Greek myth explores themes of sacrifice, divine intervention, and the transformative power of selflessness.*

At its core, the narrative underscores the human instinct to seek solutions in the face of crisis. Faced with a deadly plague, the city's leaders turn to the divine, consulting the oracle of Apollo for guidance. The gods, in their enigmatic way, prescribe a sacrifice to appease the gods of the underworld. Here, the myth delves into the eternal human struggle to comprehend and navigate the unpredictable forces that shape our existence.

The choice of the Koronides, daughters of Orion, as the sacrificial maidens adds a layer of meaning. The sisters, engaged in the mundane yet symbolic act of weaving, represent the threads of destiny and the interconnectedness of life. Their acceptance of the sacrificial fate speaks to the profound sense of duty and communal responsibility, transcending personal desires for the greater good. In doing so, they become archetypal figures embodying the timeless theme of self-sacrifice for the well-being of others.

The ritualistic nature of the maidens' sacrifice, with the piercing of perónisi and the gashing of throats, mirrors the ancient Greek tradition of blood offerings to appease the gods. However, the unexpected twist lies in the divine intervention of Persephone and Hades. Instead of descending into the depths of the underworld, the Koronides are elevated to the celestial realm, transformed into comets. This celestial metamorphosis symbolizes the transcendence of mortal limitations and the elevation of their sacrifice to a cosmic level.

The myth invites contemplation on the nature of sacrifice, the delicate balance between life and death, and the potential for divine mercy. It suggests that acts of selflessness, even in the face of seemingly insurmountable challenges, can lead to unexpected transformations and a higher state of being. The celestial ascent of the Koronides echoes the idea that noble sacrifices have a lasting impact, transcending the temporal realm and finding eternal resonance in the cosmic tapestry of existence.

Ultimately, this myth encourages reflection on the profound nature of sacrifice, the interconnectedness of life and death, and the potential for transformative redemption through selfless acts that resonate beyond the confines of mortal existence.

Persephone and Hades

In the realm of Thessalian mythology, a tale unfolds that intertwines the fates of Hades, the gloomy god of the Underworld, and Persephone, the radiant goddess of spring. The story begins in the vibrant meadows of Earth, where Persephone delighted in the beauty of blooming flowers and the sweet fragrance of nature.

One fateful day, as Persephone roamed the fields, her laughter echoed through the air, capturing the attention of Hades, who resided in the dark depths of the Underworld. Struck by the allure of her enchanting presence, Hades hatched a plan to make Persephone his own.

Under the cover of shadows, Hades emerged from the

underworld and, with a swift and stealthy movement, abducted Persephone, whisking her away to his palace. The earth trembled at the force of his action, and the once-lively meadows fell into a sudden and haunting stillness.

Persephone's mother, Demeter, the goddess of the harvest and Persephone's protector, was devastated by the disappearance of her beloved daughter. In her grief, Demeter mourned, causing the earth to wither and crops to die. The once-thriving land became a desolate realm, reflecting Demeter's sorrow.

As the days turned into weeks, Persephone found herself in the vast, cavernous halls of the Underworld. Surrounded by the shadows and echoes of the dead, she felt a profound sense of loneliness. However, Hades, captivated by her beauty and grace, sought to make her his queen.

Despite the grim surroundings, Hades treated Persephone with unexpected kindness. He adorned her with jewels crafted from the treasures of the Underworld and presented her with delicate flowers that bloomed in the darkest corners of his realm. Over time, Persephone's heart softened, and she began to see a different side of Hades.

Meanwhile, on the surface, Demeter's grief continued to cast a pall over the world. The gods, witnessing the suffering of both mother and daughter, convened to find a resolution. A compromise was reached, and it was decided that Persephone would spend part of the year in the Underworld with Hades and the remaining months on Earth with her mother.

This arrangement became the origin of the seasons. When Persephone returned to the surface, Demeter's joy transformed the barren land into a bountiful paradise, heralding the arrival of spring and summer. However, as Persephone descended into the Underworld, Demeter's sorrow plunged the world into the cold grip of autumn and winter.

And so, the tale of Hades' abduction of Persephone became a poignant story of love, compromise, and the eternal cycle of nature's changing seasons.

COMMENTARY: *The myth of Hades' abduction of Persephone carries profound symbolic meaning, reflecting themes of life, death, transformation, and the cyclical nature of the seasons. At its core, the narrative is a complex allegory that delves into both the natural world and the human experience, offering insights into the inevitability of change and the interconnectedness of opposing forces.*

The myth serves as a metaphor for the changing seasons, tying Persephone's time spent in the Underworld with the barren months of autumn and winter and her return to Earth with the vibrant seasons of spring and summer. This cyclical pattern mirrors the perpetual cycle of life, death, and rebirth observed in nature.

Hades' realm represents the afterlife, and Persephone's descent into the Underworld symbolizes the inevitability of death. However, her return to the surface signifies the cyclical renewal of life. The myth thus explores the dualistic nature of existence, where life and death are inextricably linked. Persephone's journey is one of transformation and growth. While her initial abduction causes sorrow and separation, her time in the Underworld becomes a period of self-discovery and acceptance. This theme resonates with the human experience, emphasizing the potential for personal growth and resilience even in the face of adversity.

The relationship between Hades and Persephone introduces the theme of love and compromise. Despite the unconventional circumstances of their union, there is a nuanced portrayal of Hades, challenging the stereotypical image of the god of the Underworld. The compromise struck by the gods highlights the necessity of finding balance and harmony in relationships, even when faced with opposing forces.

Demeter's grief over the loss of her daughter adds another layer to the myth. Her mourning is not merely a reflection of personal loss but also a representation of the impact of death on the living world. This maternal sorrow becomes the catalyst for the changing seasons, illustrating the profound influence of human emotions on the natural order. The myth suggests that the harmony between the Underworld and the Earth is essential for the balance of the cosmos. It underscores the interconnectedness of all things, portraying a delicate equilibrium that must be maintained for the world to flourish.

EVERY YEAR ON THE FIRST FULL MOON OF SPRING, THESSALIANS WILL GATHER AND CELEBRATE THE RETURN OF PERSEPHONE FROM HER TIME IN THE UNDERWORLD. THIS IS KNOWN AS THE FESTIVAL OF ANTHESTERIA, THE FESTIVAL OF FLOWERS.

PERSEPHONE'S PLACE ON MOUNT OLYMPUS

Persephone, for Thessalians, stands as the eternal embodiment of feminine youth and the cycle of death and rebirth. She holds a distinctive position among the divine beings of Mount Olympus. Although part of the royal court, she is not counted as an Olympian. Much like her husband Hades, Persephone tends to her divine duties and steers clear of much of the intrigue associated with her more powerful family members. She is universally loved, and her mythical presence is acknowledged by all the gods.

Persephone's place on Mount Olympus is as the daughter of Demeter, the goddess of agriculture, and Zeus, the king of the gods. As such, she is part of the Olympian Royal Court, though her time is often divided between the Earth's surface and the Underworld, where she rules alongside her husband, Hades.

While Persephone does reside on Mount Olympus for part of the year with the other gods and goddesses, her role is unique due to her dual domain over both the world of the living and the realm of the dead. This duality gives her a distinctive position among the Olympian gods, as she bridges the gap between the divine and the mortal, the light and the dark, the living and the dead.

Despite her divided time, Persephone is still recognized and honored as an Olympian goddess, with her own myths, festivals, and cults dedicated to her worship. Her presence on Mount Olympus underscores her significance in the Thessalian pantheon and her role in shaping the natural world, the cycle of life and death, and the mysteries of existence.

ATTRIBUTES OF PERSEPHONE

Persephone, the daughter of Demeter and Zeus, occupies a prominent place in Thessalian religion, embodying a complex array of attributes that resonate with both the natural world and human experience. Her multifaceted nature offers a rich tapestry of symbolism and meaning, inviting contemplation on themes of life, death, duality, empowerment, and the mysteries of existence.

One of Persephone's most renowned attributes is her association with the cycle of life and death. Her abduction by Hades and subsequent time in the Underworld symbolize the cyclical nature of existence, where life, death, and rebirth are interconnected. Her annual return from the Underworld to the Earth's surface heralds the arrival of spring, marking a time of renewal and growth. This cyclical journey mirrors the transitions and transformations that individuals experience throughout their lives, emphasizing the passage of souls between different realms or stages of existence.

Persephone's journey between the world above and the Underworld serves as a powerful metaphor for transitions and transformations. Her movement between these realms signifies the fluidity of life's transitions, as well as the potential for personal growth and change. Persephone embodies the transformative power of resilience and adaptability, inspiring individuals to embrace change and navigate life's challenges with strength and grace.

Persephone's duality is a central aspect of her character, representing the interconnectedness of opposing forces in the natural world and human experience. As the daughter of Demeter, the goddess of agriculture, Persephone symbolizes fertility, growth, and abundance. In contrast, her role as the queen of the Underworld connects her to themes of death, decay, and darkness. This dual nature underscores the balance and harmony inherent in the universe, highlighting the interplay between light and darkness, life and death, growth and decay.

Despite the circumstances of her abduction, Persephone emerges as a figure of empowerment and independence in her mythological narrative. She asserts her agency as a queen and a goddess, establishing her own domain and influence separate from her role as Hades' wife. Persephone's story celebrates the strength, resilience, and autonomy of the feminine spirit, encouraging individuals to recognize and cultivate their own inner power.

Persephone's association with the Underworld, mystery rites, and the unseen forces of the cosmos taps into humanity's fascination with the unknown, the mystical, and the spiritual realms beyond our immediate understanding. Her story invites exploration of the deeper mysteries of existence, encouraging individuals to embrace the complexities of life and seek understanding beyond the surface.

Persephone's attributes form a multifaceted portrait of a goddess who embodies the complexities and contradictions of the human experience. Her story serves as a timeless allegory, offering insights into the cyclical nature of life, the transformative power of resilience, the balance of opposing forces, the empowerment of the individual, and the enduring mysteries that shape our existence. Persephone invites us to engage with these themes, inspiring contemplation, reflection, and growth as we navigate our own journeys through life.

PERSEPHONE'S INFLUENCES

Persephone's influence on human existence is multifaceted, encompassing, as explained above, themes of life's cycles, duality, empowerment, mysticism, and connection to nature. Her mythological narrative and attributes offer a rich source of wisdom, inspiration, and contemplation, guiding individuals on their journeys of self-discovery, growth, and understanding of the interconnectedness of all things. Persephone's timeless relevance underscores her enduring significance in shaping human consciousness and the cultural tapestry of humanity.

PERSEPHONE'S CLERGY

Priests and priestesses of Persephone should ideally embody qualities that reflect her multifaceted nature and the themes associated with her worship. These include wisdom and insight, empathy, and a strong sense of communal bonding.

Thessalian priests and priestesses of Persephone serve a vital role in guiding, supporting, and inspiring followers on their spiritual journeys. By embodying the attributes of their chosen goddess, they can effectively serve their community, honor Persephone's legacy, and help individuals connect with the profound wisdom, empowerment, and transformational potential inherent in her worship.

They are also responsible for the conducting of two major Thessalian festivals – the Anthesteria (Persephone's return) and the Thesmophoria (Persephone's descent). These two festivals are crucial to the fabric of Thessalian religious society and are celebrated by all Thessalian groups even if they do not have within their ranks devoted clergy to the goddess Persephone.

These two festivals mark the cycles of death and rebirth and are times of remembrance of our ancestors, our beloved dead, and a stark reminder of our own mortality and eventual rebirth.

PERSEPHONE'S

KOMBOSKINI

As we delve deeper into the rich tapestry of Greek spirituality, we encounter a fascinating and deeply symbolic tradition known as the "Komboskini." This ancient practice has woven its way through Greek culture for centuries, offering a unique insight into the spiritual pursuits of its practitioners.

ORIGINS AND SIGNIFICANCE
The word "Komboskini" finds its roots in the Greek word "*komboskio*," which means "knot" or "bead." It is often referred to as a "prayer chaplet". Much like its counterparts in other faiths, such as the Catholic rosary or the Islamic Misbaha, the Komboskini is a tool for devout Thessalians to engage in contemplative prayer and meditation.

The Thessalian komboskini consists of a string of beads, typically made from various materials like wood, stone, or even precious gems, strung together to form a loop. It contains 49 beads that serve as counters for the repetition of prayers or mantras.

SPIRITUAL PRACTICE
In the Thessalian religious traditions, the Komboskini is used as a means to recite a variety of mantras. The devotee holds the Komboskini in one hand while using the fingers to move from one bead to the next, repeating the prayer with each bead. This rhythmic and meditative practice enables the individual to focus their mind and heart on the deity to whom they are directing their prayer, inviting a sense of inner peace and communion with the divine.

SYMBOLISM AND MEDITATION

The symbolism of the Komboskini is rich and multifaceted. Each bead is seen as a knot that binds the soul to the divine. As the practitioner advances through the beads, it represents a journey of spiritual progression and growth.

Moreover, the Komboskini is considered a symbol of unity and interconnectedness. The circular nature of the prayer chaplet reflects the eternal cycle of life, death, and rebirth, and the interconnectedness of all living beings. It is a reminder of the cyclical and timeless nature of the divine.

PERSONAL AND COMMUNAL PRACTICE

The Komboskini is not solely reserved for individual spiritual practice. It is often used in communal settings, such as temple rites, where Thessalians will gather to pray together. The repetitive recitation of the mantra on the prayer chaplet not only deepens personal devotion but also creates a sense of unity and shared commitment among the participants.

The Greek Komboskini is a cherished aspect of Thessalian spirituality, a tangible and symbolic tool that aids individuals

on their journey of devotion. Through its use, Thessalians seek a deeper connection with the divine, personal growth, and a profound sense of unity with the world and with each other. It stands as a testament to the enduring and diverse spiritual traditions that continue to thrive within Greek culture.

THE SACRED LOROS

In the realm of Thessalian spirituality, there exists a profound ritual that weaves threads of devotion and symbolism into the very fabric of one's connection to a deity. This practice, rooted in symbolism and reverence, is the art of braiding colored cords to symbolize an individual's connection to a god or goddess. It is an act of spiritual significance that weaves together the believer's life with the divine, much like an ethereal umbilical cord. This sacred cord is called a Λωρος – Loros.

This Thessalian custom is an intricate and sacred process, known as a *Lambano Rite* or *Rite of Reception*. The core of the ritual serves as a rite of passage for those who wish to deepen their spiritual connection to a particular deity. It signifies the individual's acceptance and commitment to the deity's teachings, values, and guidance.

At the heart of this ritual are the colorful cords. These cords are made of natural materials such as silk or wool. Every god, goddess, spirit, and hero has a particular combination of colors, representing qualities or attributes associated with the chosen power.

The cords are braided together by tying one end of the cords to an image or statue of the deity and braiding to create a single, unified strand that is the height of the devotee. This act of weaving is considered a symbol of the union between the individual and the god or goddess. It mimics the creation of a spiritual umbilical cord, linking the two together in a bond of devotion and shared purpose.

During this ritual, the practitioner recites prayers or mantras that invoke the presence and blessings of the chosen deity. When the cord is completed, it is soaked in a special herbal infusion that will steep it with spiritual energy and intention.

Upon completion, the cord becomes a tangible representation of the divine connection. Its vibrant colors and intricate pattern tell the story of the spiritual journey it signifies.

The cord is usually worn over the shoulders of the practitioner as a symbol of their connection to the deity. It serves as a daily reminder of their commitment, values, and spiritual path. Some choose to wear it discreetly, under their clothing, while others proudly display it as a badge of honor and faith.

The braided cord, as a spiritual umbilical cord, symbolizes the ongoing nurturing and sustenance of the individual's connection with the god or goddess. It serves as a lifeline, linking the mortal to the divine, and providing guidance, support, and strength along their spiritual journey.

PERSEPHONE'S SACRED LOROS

Persephone's Sacred Cord is braided with the colors: Black, Green, and Red.

TRADITIONAL OFFERINGS TO PERSEPHONE

In the Thessalian religious tradition, the reverence for Persephone takes on a unique form, where the mystical rites and religious expressions are presented as a ritualized offering to the goddess of life, death, and renewal. These profound ceremonies encapsulate the belief that the very essence of mystical and ritualistic endeavors, along with the profound energy arising from such rites, is consecrated to Persephone herself.

Reflecting the multifaceted character of Persephone, devotees express their devotion through various offerings that symbolize the goddess's qualities and dominion. Items such as pomegranates, grains, and floral wreaths stand as customary votive offerings to Persephone, often crafted with meticulous skill and placed in her temple as symbols of beauty and rebirth. Another favored votive offering is the presentation of wreaths adorned with herbs or other symbols of nature, which are elegantly displayed over her statues or hung about the walls of her temples and shrines, signifying the enduring cycle of life, death, and renewal.

In a unique homage to the goddess of the underworld and the changing seasons, dedicating performances, such as ritualistic dances or seasonal celebrations, is considered a fitting and honorable offering. This act not only showcases the devotion of the participants to Persephone but also underscores the natural cycles and transformative power intrinsic to the goddess's sphere of influence.

The Thessalian rituals and offerings to Persephone become a celebration of the enduring dance of life, death, and rebirth inspired by the goddess of the underworld and fertility. These acts of veneration not only honor Persephone's divine attributes but also embody the unyielding power of nature, resilience, and the mystical spirit that resonates through the annals of Thessalian tradition.

SACRED ANIMALS

Persephone holds certain creatures in the highest esteem within her divine realm. Among these sacred animals, deer, bats, myna birds, and all talking birds stand out as particularly cherished and revered by the goddess. These creatures encapsulate qualities that resonate with the essence of Persephone, and as such, their presence, parts, and symbols are frequently offered to the goddess as tokens of devotion.

Deer, graceful and elusive, symbolizes the delicate balance between life and death that is integral to Persephone's domain. Their gentle presence and serene spirit mirror the goddess's association with the changing seasons, renewal, and the mystical unknown. Devotees may offer parts of deer, such as antlers or hooves, or even small sculptures of these animals, as a gesture of homage to Persephone. In doing so, they seek to invoke her nurturing spirit and the transformative energy that pervades her sacred rites and rituals.

Bats, with their nocturnal and transformative nature, embody the mysteries and transitions associated with Persephone's character. Devotees may present symbols or images of bats as offerings, acknowledging the transformative and mystical force that Persephone represents in matters of growth and renewal.

Pigs are also sacred to Persephone, as it is said in myth, that when Hades abducted the young goddess, several pigs fell into the chasm he opened in the earth and so from that day forth, pigs were offered to Her.

Myna birds and all talking birds, known for their communicative abilities and symbolic significance, align closely with Persephone's attributes as the goddess of transitions and communication between realms. Their vocal nature symbolizes the connection between the mortal world and the divine, embodying the guidance and mystical qualities inherent in Persephone's realm. Devotees may offer feathers, or even figurines of these birds, to Persephone. In doing so, they express a desire for the guidance and transformative energy associated with the goddess in navigating life's transitions and mysteries.

These creatures, each possessing unique qualities, become vessels through which devotees seek to connect with the divine attributes of Persephone. The rituals and offerings involving deer, bats, pigs, myna birds, and all talking birds become a celebration of the goddess' multifaceted nature, embodying the qualities of renewal, transformation, communication, and mystical insight that resonate through the divine realm of Persephone.

SACRED PLANTS

Amidst the array of sacred plants, the Asphodel, Wheat, Cherry trees, and Pomegranate trees hold unique places of significance in the affection of Persephone. Among the Thessalians, these plants are revered for their roles in representing the cycles of life, death, rebirth, fertility, and transformation associated with Persephone's domain.

Inhabited by nature spirits, known as dryads, these trees and plants are regarded with a sense of sacred respect. Disturbing them without proper reverence may disrupt the balance and invite unintended consequences from these mystical beings. The Thessalians, recognizing the enchanting qualities of these plants, utilize their branches, fruits, and seeds in their rituals and offerings, crafting wreaths, and adornments to honor Persephone's connection to the natural world.

Beyond their roles in magical rites, these plants find places in Thessalian customs and traditions. Wheat and Asphodel, for instance, symbolize the cycles of life, death, and rebirth, with Asphodel particularly associated with the afterlife and the Elysian Fields. Cherry and Pomegranate trees, on the other hand, represent fertility, abundance, and the mysteries of the underworld, especially the pomegranate's seeds linking Persephone to her time in the Underworld.

These plants, each possessing unique qualities and symbolism, become vessels through which devotees seek to connect with the divine attributes of Persephone. The rituals and offerings involving Asphodel, Wheat, Cherry trees, and Pomegranate trees become a celebration of the goddess' multifaceted nature, embodying the qualities of renewal, transformation, fertility, and the cycles that resonate through Persephone's divine realm.

ALTERNATIVE SACRIFICES

In the tradition of offering to the gods and goddesses, a significant aspect to consider is the choice of animals as an offering. This practice, rooted in ancient Greek customs, symbolizes devotion and respect to the Divine Powers. However, the Thessalian alternative, which departs from the practice of animal sacrifice, involves the filling of gourds, melons, or coconuts with red wine and meticulously painting them in the sacred colors of the deity to whom they are to be offered. These wine-filled offerings are then placed upon the altar and chopped open using a special short sword known as a Harpe.

This modern approach to sacrifice aligns with the evolving perspectives on animal welfare and ethical considerations, offering a way to honor the goddess while adhering to a more contemporary and compassionate ethos. It is a testament to the adaptability of religious practices to reflect changing values and beliefs, all while maintaining the core principles of reverence and devotion to the gods.

OFFERING WINE-FILLED COCONUTS AT A THESSALIAN FESTIVAL

Characteristics of Persephone and Her Worshipers

Those individuals whom Persephone chooses to be her devotees tend to embody several key characteristics that reflect the goddess's profound influence on human existence. They recognize the transformative power of change and are attuned to the natural ebb and flow of existence, finding renewal in each cycle and understanding and embracing the cyclical nature of life, death, and rebirth.

Children of Persephone also often embody the goddess' dual nature. These individuals strive to harmonize opposing forces within themselves and the world around them. They appreciate the balance between light and darkness, growth and decay, fostering a deeper understanding of life's complexities, tending to be both colorful, and gothic in their character.

Inspired by Persephone's journey from abduction to empowerment, devotees cultivate strength, resilience, and agency in their lives. They face challenges with courage and determination, asserting their autonomy and shaping their destinies with purpose.

Drawn to Persephone's association with the mystical and the unseen, devotees have a deep curiosity about the spiritual realms beyond our immediate understanding. They engage in introspection, seeking meaning, purpose, and connection in the mysteries of existence.

Revering Persephone's connection to the earth and its cycles, devotees nurture a strong bond with nature. They respect and protect the environment, recognizing its intrinsic value and the importance of sustainability in sustaining life.

In essence, a devotee of Persephone embodies a holistic approach to life, embracing its cycles, complexities, and mysteries. They find inspiration, wisdom, and guidance in Persephone's mythological narrative, allowing her timeless relevance to shape their journeys of self-discovery, growth, and interconnectedness with the world around them.

EPITHETS OF PERSEPHONE:

An epithet, in the context of deity and divine reverence, takes the form of an adjective or descriptive phrase that encapsulates a distinctive quality or attribute of the deity or being in question. This practice of assigning epithets to gods and goddesses is an integral facet of ancient religious traditions, serving as a means to precisely articulate and evoke the particular aspect or essence of the deity one seeks to invoke for aid or guidance.

Each deity within the pantheon boasts a rich tapestry of specific epithets, each carefully tailored to delineate the unique facets of their character and domain, thereby allowing practitioners to draw upon their divine qualities with clarity and purpose. These epithets serve as a sacred lexicon, enabling devotees to navigate the multifaceted realm of the divine and engage with it in a manner that aligns with their specific needs and intentions.

- Κορη — *Kore* – Maiden or Girl
- Πραξιδικη— *Praxidike* – Exacter of Justice
- Ἁγνη— *Hagne* – Holy-One
- Χθονια— *Chthoniai* – Of the Underworld
- Ανθόκορυς— *Anthokoros* – Flower-crowned
- Σωτειρα— *Soteira* - Savior
- Δαειρα— *Daeira* – Knowing One
- Μεγαλα Θεα— *Megala Thea* – Great Goddess
- Καρποφορος— *Karpophoros* – Fruit-Bearer

PRAYERS, HYMNS, & SONGS TO PERSEPHONE

Individuals who have been initiated into the Thessalian faith can amplify the potency of their rituals and endeavors devoted to Persephone by reciting these prayers and hymns, as well as by singing these sacred songs to the goddess. These reverent expressions of devotion draw upon a rich tradition, with some dating back to ancient times and others representing more contemporary creations. Regardless of their origin, all are efficacious in invoking the immense power of the Goddess of Spring and Death.

THESSALIAN HYMN TO PERSEPHONE *(C.2001 C.E. - Monte Plaisance)*

O Persephone, radiant Queen of the Underworld, Daughter of Demeter, Goddess of the fruitful earth, You who dance between light and shadow, Guiding souls through life's eternal cycle.

In your embrace, we find the mysteries of existence, The delicate balance of life, death, and rebirth, Your journey from darkness to light, Bringing forth spring's blossoms, and renewing the earth.

Champion of resilience, beacon of empowerment, You who rose from adversity, a symbol of strength, Teach us to face challenges with grace, embrace our inner power, and shape our destinies.

Mistress of the unseen, guardian of the mystical, You who hold the keys to the hidden realms, Guide us through the shadows, reveal the secrets, Illuminate the path to wisdom and enlightenment.

Protector of nature, symbol of fertility, You who nurture the earth's cycles and growth, Remind us of our bond with the natural world, Inspire us to respect, cherish, and sustain its beauty.

O Persephone, hear our hymn, feel our devotion, Bless us with your wisdom, grace, and love, Guide us on our journey of self-discovery, And lead us towards unity, harmony, and eternal light.

Hail Persephone, Goddess of life's profound mysteries, We honor you, we praise you, we adore you, In your divine presence, we find inspiration, Forever grateful for your timeless guidance and love.

ORPHIC HYMN TO PERSEPHONE *(Greek hymns C3rd B.C. to 2nd A.D.)*

Daughter of Zeus, Persephone divine, come, blessed queen, and to these rites incline: only-begotten, Haides' honored wife, O venerable Goddess, source of life: 'tis thine in earth's profundities to dwell, fast by the wide and dismal gates of hell. Zeus' holy offspring, of a beauteous mien, Praxidike, subterranean queen. Erinyes' source, fair-haired, whose frame proceeds from Zeus' ineffable and secret seeds. Mother of Zagreus, sonorous, divine, and many-formed, the parent of the vine.

Associate of the Horai, essence bright,
all-ruling virgin, bearing heavenly light.
With fruits abounding, of a bounteous mind,
horned, and alone desired by those of mortal kind.
O vernal queen, whom grassy plains delight,
sweet to the smell, and pleasing to the sight:
whose holy form in budding fruits we view,
earth's vigorous offspring of a various hue:
espoused in autumn, life and death alone
to wretched mortals from thy power is known:
for thine the task , according to thy will,
life to produce, and all that lives to kill.
Hear, blessed Goddess, send a rich increase
of various fruits from earth, with lovely peace:
send health with gentle hand, and crown my life
with blest abundance, free from noisy strife;
last in extreme old age the prey of death,
dismiss me willing to the realms beneath,
to thy fair palace and the blissful plains
where happy spirits dwell, and Haides reigns.

THESSALIAN CHANT OF PERSEPHONE

This simple chant is repeated in unison until the power of
Persephone is felt. It is used as an invocation and as an
offering.

> *Queen of the Stars and Queen of the Dead.*
> *Queen of the Horns and Queen of Fire.*
> *Harken to this sacred sign.*
> *Grant us now what we desire.*
> *Queen of the Dead, Queen of the Light.*
> *Flame that warms the coldest night.*
> *Bring to us a waxing light.*
> *Grant to us your Holy Sight.*

THE WHEEL OF MAGIC (TO RAISE POWER FOR SPELL WORK)

Fire flame and fire burn,
> Make the wheel of magic turn.

Work the will for which I pray
> I Ω H Ω I H A (pronounced eye-oh-ee-oh-eye-ee-ay)

Water heat and water boil,
> Make the wheel of magic toil,

Work the will for which I pray
> I Ω H Ω I H A (pronounced eye-oh-ee-oh-eye-ee-ay)

Air breath and air blow,
> Make the wheel of magic go,

Work the will for which I pray
> I Ω H Ω I H A (pronounced eye-oh-ee-oh-eye-ee-ay)

Earth without and earth within,
> Make the wheel of magic spin.

Work the will for which I pray,
> I Ω H Ω I H A (pronounced eye-oh-ee-oh-eye-ee-ay)

NOTE: *This chant should be repeated over and over with the clapping of your hands. Each time say it faster until the tempo is so fast that you cannot go any faster. This will raise immense power to help work your spell.*

PERSEPHONE'S PLACE IN THE MODERN HOME

Persephone holds a revered and crucial role in the Thessalian religion, but within the modern household, her function is mostly limited to times when we have lost a loved one. Religiously, she is seen as the Queen of the Underworld and as a judge of the souls of the dead once they have reached their place in the underworld.

Whenever a household has lost a loved one to death, a large black vase is placed outside, just to the left of the front door. On the vase is painted with the deceased's name, Hades' Bident staff and it is either wreathed with red poppies or red poppies are painted onto it. There are certain members of Thessalian Clergy who may not enter a home wherein someone has died for at least 40 days in order to avoid contact with any residual energy of death and this vase serves both as a temporary shrine to Persephone and Hades and as a notice to any clergy who may be visiting. Also, the home must be cleansed by burning sulfur throughout the house and then a thorough sweeping and mopping with a special floor wash called Glory Water to remove any traces of death that may be lingering in the home. that death has visited the home.

Thessalian Clergy will, upon the death of citizen, begin a series of rituals that take 40 days to complete. These rituals involve many petitions to both Persephone and Hades, to be kind to the deceased and help them to find their way in the underworld.

Persephone Rituals and Spells

Thessalians have adapted ancient rites and mystic traditions to seek the favor and blessings of the goddess Persephone. These modern rituals draw on the mythology of Persephone as the goddess of the underworld and spring growth and so the spells associated with her often center on themes of transformation, rebirth, and the cycles of life and death.

Here are some mystical spells that could be performed with her assistance. Enchantments and invocations are woven into these contemporary ceremonies, beseeching Persephone's transformative and powerful influence to ensure the inspiring power of rebirth, resilience, and growth of Thessalian devotees. Devotees implore Persephone to open them up to the reception of changes, usher in blessings and growth, and bless their lives and endeavors. In these modern adaptations, the timeless devotion to Persephone is manifested through tangible actions that embrace the essence of magic and deep contemplation, further deepening the connection between the goddess and those who continue to revere her in contemporary contexts.

Spell for Transformation and Personal Growth

This spell for Transformation and Personal Growth is designed to invoke personal change and development, inspired by Persephone's cyclical journey between the underworld and the living world.

ITEMS YOU WILL NEED:
- Pomegranate seeds
- A black candle (for the underworld)
- A white candle (for rebirth)
- A mirror
- A small bowl of soil

PREPARATION:

Find a quiet place where you won't be disturbed. Set up your altar with the black and white candles, and the mirror. Place the pomegranate seeds and the bowl of soil on a separate table away from the mirror.

Take a purification bath using either sea salt or Natron salts[1] immediately before performing this rite. After cleansing, dress in a clean white outfit (medical scrubs are perfect for this) and approach the altar.

Light the black candle first, invoking Persephone's presence in the underworld by saying:

> *"Persephone, Queen of the Underworld, guardian of the hidden realms, I call upon your wisdom and strength."*

Then light the white candle, representing her return to the living world and say:

> *"Persephone, Bringer of Spring, radiant Queen of renewal, I call upon your vibrant energy."*

Sit comfortably and hold the pomegranate seeds or the whole pomegranate in your hands. Close your eyes and take deep breaths, imagining the seeds as symbols of potential and new growth.

When you have the image of growth firmly in your mind, recite the following prayer:

> *"Persephone, Queen of the Underworld and Bringer of Spring, guide me through the darkness and into the light. Help me to transform and grow, as you do each year. Guide me through the shadows and unveil the mysteries within. Bestow upon me your protection and insight as I journey through the depths. Hail, Persephone, goddess of transformation and rebirth."*

Look into the mirror and imagine the reflection you see as the opposing side of you, containing all things that you wish to remove. When the reflection holds all the things you wish to remove, close your eyes and turn away. Leave that version of

---

[1] Natron Salts can be purchased through Church of Thessaly.

yourself in the mirror (underworld) and extinguish the black candle. Take up the white candle and walk away from the mirror to the table where you have the pomegranate seeds and the soil.

Take the pomegranate seeds and plant them in the bowl of soil. As you do, say:

"As these seeds transform and grow, so too shall I."

Meditate for a moment on the growth you want to establish in your life, the white candle should be left to burn out on its own.[2]

NOTE: The bowl of soil should be placed on a windowsill or outdoors until the seeds sprout. Once the seeds have sprouted, the spell is done. It is not necessary for the seeds to grow into a full tree for this spell to work, they only need to sprout. However, if you have the space and would like to transfer the sprouts to the earth and grow a full pomegranate tree, it would be an excellent offering to Persephone.

---

[2] Always exercise caution with this. You should not leave a candle burning unattended, so stay in the room while it burns. If you must leave the room, you can place the candle inside of a large cooking pot with a small amount of water in the bottom. This will serve to extinguish the candle should it tip over or some other unforeseen incident occur.

SPELL FOR RENEWAL AND NEW BEGINNINGS

This spell is performed to bring about new beginnings and fresh starts, inspired by Persephone's emergence from the underworld each spring.

ITEMS YOU WILL NEED:

- Fresh flowers (preferably spring flowers like daffodils or crocuses)
- A green candle
- A bowl of fresh water
- A small piece of paper and a pen

PREPARATION:

Arrange the flowers, candle, and bowl of water on your altar or ritual space. Take a cleansing bath and dress in your ritual robes or clothes.

Approach the altar with solemnity and reverence. Light the green candle, which symbolizes growth and new beginnings. Spend a few moments in silent meditation, focusing on the sense of renewal and new opportunities.

Take up the pen and on the piece of paper, write down the new beginnings or changes you wish to bring into your life. Fold the paper several times, always folding it towards you. Hold the folded paper in your palms and recite the following prayer:

"Persephone, Goddess of Spring and Renewal, bless these intentions with your power. As you emerge from the darkness, so too shall these new beginnings come to light."

Dip the paper into the bowl of water, letting the water absorb the energy of your intentions. Then sprinkle a few drops of the water over the flowers, symbolizing the nourishment and growth of your desires. Now drink the water, thus consuming the spell and making it a part of you.

Let the candle burn for a while longer as you reflect on the spell's purpose, then extinguish it, thanking Persephone for her assistance.

Relight the candle every day and focus your mind on achieving your goals. Recite the prayer again if you like.

SPELL FOR PROTECTION AND GUIDANCE IN DARKNESS

To seek protection and guidance during difficult or uncertain times, invoking Persephone's strength as the Queen of the Underworld.

ITEMS YOU WILL NEED:
- A black tourmaline or obsidian stone
- A purple candle (for spiritual protection)
- Dried lavender and sage
- A small red sachet or pouch

PREPARATION:
Place the stone, candle, and dried herbs on your altar. Take a cleansing bath and dress in your ritual robes or clothes.

Approach the altar and light the purple candle, asking for Persephone's protective presence.

> *"Persephone, Queen of the Underworld, guardian of the hidden realms, I call upon your wisdom and strength."*

Hold the stone in your dominant hand. Focus your attention on your head and try to 'feel' the stone's grounding and protective energy. It should feel like a steady pulse, almost like a fast heartbeat in the palm of your hand.

Place the dried lavender and sage into the small pouch along with the stone, infusing it with your protective intentions. Close your eyes, take three deep breaths and pray:

> "*Divine Persephone, Queen of the Underworld and Guardian of the Mysteries, in this hour, I call upon your presence and your power. Bless this charm bag with your protective grace, Infuse it with the strength of your underworld domain, Shielding me from harm, guiding me through shadows.*
>
> *Persephone, Keeper of the Hidden Realms, As you navigate the depths, so too may this charm, Be a beacon of safety in times of darkness, A ward against negativity, a shield against fear.*
>
> *With each stitch, with each herb and stone enclosed, May your divine energy flow, your wisdom bestowed. May this charm bag be a sacred vessel of your blessing, A talisman of protection, a token of your favor.*
>
> *As I carry it upon my person, let it be a constant reminder, Of your presence, your strength, your unwavering care. Persephone, hear my prayer, grant me this boon, And may your protective powers surround me soon.*
>
> *Hail Persephone, Queen of Protection and Renewal, Blessed be your name, now and always.*
>
> *Selathae!*[3]

Place the sachet at the base of the purple candle until the candle burns out completely. Now you can carry the saschet with you as a talisman of Persephone's protection and guidance.

---

[3] Selathae is a Thessalian ritual term that essentially means "So be it". It is pronounced seh-LAH-thay.

PERSEPHONE'S FAVORITE RECIPES

As a goddess of both Springtime and Death, Persephone cherishes the vibrancy of life and also the sanctity of death. As a deity, her food offerings lean hearty dishes filled with flavor. Creating a ceremonial banquet to celebrate Persephone and symbolically passing the dishes and offerings over your body before presenting them to her can serve as a significant ritual of purification. This age-old practice acts as a potent method to banish negativity and call upon the divine favor of the goddess, ushering in positive energies to enrich both your personal life and your home.

KEFTEDES ME RODI (MEATBALLS IN POMEGRANATE SAUCE)

These Greek Meatballs in Pomegranate sauce, are a perfect offering for Persehpone.

The Greek word for meatballs is Keftedes. These meatballs are served in a delicious pomegranate sauce.

INGREDIENTS:
- 2 lbs mixed ground pork and beef
- 1 cup of soaked bread (crust removed before soaking) and squeezed to remove water
- 1 onion, blended with 1 tbsp olive oil
- 2 large eggs
- 1 tbsp dried oregano
- ½ cup of minced fresh parsley
- 2 tablespoons dried mint or ¼ cup minced fresh mint
- 1/4 tablespoon dried dill or 2 tbsp fresh dill
- 1 teaspoon of garlic powder or 1 clove fresh garlic, minced
- 1 tbsp salt
- 1/2 tsp freshly ground pepper
- Flour for dredging (about 1 cup)
- Olive oil for frying

For the sauce
- 1 cup of dry red wine
- Seeds of 2 pomegranates, reserve 2 tablespoons of seeds and the rest make into juice (about 1/4 cup)
- 1/2 tablespoonful ground nutmeg
- 1 bay leaf
- 6 - 8 plums, pitted and sliced thin
- 1/4 cup milk
- 1 tbsp all-purpose flour

INSTRUCTIONS:
1. Grate the onion on a grater or puree it in a food processor. If it does not puree easily add a tbsp of olive oil.

2. In a large bowl, mix the ground beef and pork with the bread, eggs, onion, garlic, oregano, mint, parsley, dill, and salt and pepper.

3. Refrigerate for half an hour.

4. Form into oval or round meatballs.

5. In a large skillet, fry the meatballs in the olive oil over medium heat, turning them so that they cook on all sides.

6. Remove the meatballs from the skillet and cover to keep them warm while you make the pomegranate sauce.

7. Add the wine to the skillet and bring to a boil, scraping up the brown bits from frying pan; boil until reduced by half, about 5 minutes.

8. Cut the pomegranates in half and reserve 2 tablespoonful of seeds.

9. Very gently squeeze each half of the pomegranate until you get 1/4 cup of juice.

10. Add the juice to the skillet with the nutmeg, bay leaf, and plum slices. Continue to cook on high heat until the plum slices are soft.

11. Dissolve the flour in the milk and add it to the sauce.

12. Stir for 3 - 4 minutes or until the sauce becomes thick.

13. Return the meatballs to the pan and toss with the sauce. Season with salt and pepper, if needed.

14. Garnish with the reserved pomegranate seeds and serve with rice or mashed potatoes.

GREEK BRAISED PORK

This pork dish is a wonderful balance of sweet and savory so often found in Greek cuisine. 'Balance' is the key word as it has just the right amount of sweetness and pairs well with the pork. This dish symbolizes the dualistic nature of

Persephone as both Queen of the Underworld and Goddess of Spring.

INGREDIENTS:

- 5 to 6 pounds or boneless country pork ribs, trimmed, cut into 2-inch pieces and patted dry
- ¼ cup olive oil
- 1 large red onion, halved and thinly sliced
- 1 cup dry white wine
- 2 tablespoons minced fresh rosemary, divided
- 3 bay leaves
- 2 teaspoons dried oregano
- 1 tablespoon fennel seeds
- ½ cup honey, divided
- 1 tablespoon grated orange zest (~ 1 orange)
- ½ cup orange juice (~ 2 to 3 oranges)
- 3 tablespoons finely chopped fresh oregano
- 2 tablespoons apple cider vinegar
- Sea salt and ground black pepper

INSTRUCTIONS:

1. Heat the oven to 325°F with a rack in the middle position.

2. Season the pork with salt and pepper.

3. In a large (at least 7-quart) Dutch oven over medium-high heat, heat the oil.

4. Set aside about ¼ of the pork. Brown the remaining pieces of pork in batches. Add pork pieces in an even layer (be careful not to crowd them) and cook without stirring until well browned, about 7 minutes. Using tongs, flip the pieces and cook without stirring until well browned on the second side, about 5 minutes. Transfer to a medium bowl and repeat until you've browned about ¾ of the pork, adding more oil if needed. Add the remaining ¼ pork to the bowl – it does not need to be browned.

5. Reduce the heat to medium and add the onion and ¼ teaspoon Kosher salt to the pot. Cover and cook, stirring occasionally, until softened, about 3 to 5 minutes.

6. Add the wine and cook, scraping up any browned bits, until most of the liquid has evaporated, about 5 minutes.

7. Stir in 1 tablespoon rosemary, bay leaves, dried oregano, fennel seeds and ¼ cup honey.

8. Return the pork and any juices to the pot, pour in ¾ cup water, and stir.

9. Cover, transfer to the oven and cook until a skewer inserted into a piece of pork meets no resistance, about 2 to 2-1/2 hours. Check at 2 hours and cook longer if needed.

10. Using a slotted spoon, transfer the pork to a large bowl and cover to keep.

11. Tilt the pot to pool the cooking liquid to one side, then use a wide spoon to skim off and discard as much fat as possible.

12. Stir in the orange juice and remaining ¼ cup honey. Bring to a boil over high heat, then reduce to medium heat. Cook, stirring often, until a spatula drawn through the liquid leaves a trail and the liquid has reduced by about half, about 10 minutes.

13. Remove pot from heat. Stir in the orange zest, remaining 1 tablespoon rosemary, fresh oregano and vinegar.

14. Return the pork to the pot and stir to coat with the sauce. Taste and season with Kosher salt and pepper.

15. Serve immediately or let cool and refrigerate until ready to serve. Reheat pork over low heat, covered, for 10 to 15 minutes. Pork will keep, refrigerated for 3 days or frozen for up to 3 months.

SESAME HONEY BARS (PASTELI) RECIPE

Pasteli is a delightful treat that graces the modern tables of Greece and is readily available throughout the country. It's a sesame-based candy that serves as the ancient counterpart to today's energy bars. This straightforward recipe allows you to craft these delectable bars, suitable for offering to all of the gods and equally enjoyable for personal consumption.

INGREDIENTS:

- 220g honey (7.5 oz.)
- 220g sesame seeds (7.5 oz.)
- A pinch of salt
- Zest of 1 medium-sized lemon

INSTRUCTIONS:

1. To begin crafting this Greek honey sesame bars (Pasteli) recipe, commence by toasting the sesame seeds. Place a frying pan over high heat and introduce the sesame seeds. Toast them for 2-3 minutes, or until they achieve a golden hue without becoming too brown. Once done, remove the sesame seeds from the pan and set them aside. Proceed with the remainder of the recipe promptly to keep the sesame seeds warm.

2. Alternatively, you can spread the sesame seeds in a pan and toast them in the oven at 375°F.

3. In the same pan, add the honey and bring it to a boil until it begins to foam. Include a pinch of salt and the toasted sesame seeds. Reduce the heat to medium and stir continuously using a wooden spoon for approximately 3-5 minutes, until the mixture develops a delightful color. Take care not to overcook it.

4. Remove the pan from the heat and stir in the lemon

zest.

5. Line a round pan (8.5 inches in diameter) with parchment paper and pour in the mixture. Exercise caution not to touch it, as it will be extremely hot. Utilize a spoon to evenly spread the mixture within the pan.

6. Allow the pasteli to cool for about 20 minutes, and then proceed to cut it into portions. It's recommended to cut it before it cools completely, as it becomes harder to slice when fully cooled. Enjoy your homemade pasteli!

THE PYXIS OF PERSEPHONE

The pyxis, also known as a tsikali, is a sacred vessel dedicated to a specific deity in the Thessalian religion. Within this vessel, precious items that hold significance to the god or goddess are carefully placed. These items may include stones, herbs, animal parts, and more, some of which can be challenging or costly to acquire. On a theurgic level, the pyxis establishes a physical connection through the laws of resonance, which, when activated through ritual, transforms it into a sacred object that attracts the energies of the divine power. This sacred vessel serves as a physical abode for these energies, effectively materializing the deity, and allowing worshippers to interact with the divine power on a more tangible level—speaking with them, touching them, or even offering sustenance. This sensory engagement enhances the richness of spiritual experiences in Thessalian religion.

The pyxis is personified, making communication with the god or goddess more accessible. Its creation is guided by a deep understanding of the deity's personality and the historical context to which it is dedicated. Thessalian Adepts invest considerable effort in constructing the pyxis, engaging in months of meditation and ritual to establish a common ground for interaction with the divinity. Over time, the pyxis evolves into a living entity endowed with speech, emotions, and autonomy, capable of acting independently of human intervention. It can counsel, bestow favor, seek retribution for wrongs, punish impudence, request rituals, influence events in the worshiper's life, and perform countless other activities.

WHAT THE PYXIS REPRESENTS

The pyxis lays the foundation for worshipers to enter the sacred realm of Thessalian religion. Its power resides in its specific form with fixed contours, filled with various elements that remain indistinct to the uninitiated eye. Many pyxides (*plural of pyxis*) bear the marks of soot from burnt offerings, incense, and libations. Some are coated in colored waxes, melted from candle offerings burned on top of them. Offerings accumulate around it, revealing feathers, bones, horns, or other items, allowing the practitioner to observe the "mysteries of existence." This amalgamation of materiality connects the divine powers within it to mortals who come into contact with it, reinforcing the principles cherished by Thessalians—forces of nature, the regenerative energies of life, and death, and the mysteries that encompass existence.

The pyxis is held in the highest regard among Thessalians, yet few will possess one; primarily since their creation is expensive and difficult. This revered object can exert a significant influence over the personal lives of initiates, guiding their behavior. During rituals, the pyxis can induce a phenomenon called Katoche, wherein a worshiper becomes overtaken by the power of the divinity. In this state, the god or goddess may speak through the worshiper, providing advice on matters of importance such as limiting alcohol consumption, changing jobs, avoiding certain individuals, concluding business deals, and more.

THE CREATION OF A PYXIS

The creation of a pyxis is an intricate process that involves intense rituals, performed exclusively by Thessalian Adepts. However, in certain cases, the divine may decree the necessity of a pyxis or directly instruct a worshiper to craft one. In such instances, the worshiper embarks on a quest to gather the required ingredients for the pyxis.

The pyxis is composed of three levels: Θεμελιο (feet, foundation), Ουσια (heart, essence), and Κεφαλι (head, driving force). The Heart of the Pyxis is formed by collecting 24 ingredients over time, which are subsequently inspected and approved by the Thessalian Adept through the Oracle of Hermes. Once all the items are deemed acceptable, the ritual of creation can commence.

While anyone can gather the heart ingredients, only a Thessalian Adept can complete the creation of the pyxis. It is the adept's responsibility to craft the vessel for the pyxis, the Feet, and the Head. The Feet of the Pyxis comprises various ingredients that vary according to the deity being sought through the Pyxis. These ingredients are sealed into the base of the vessel with wax. The Heart is placed atop this foundation, and the Head is also fashioned by the Adept, incorporating additional ingredients. This elaborate process can span several months.

INGREDIENTS FOR THE PERSEPHONE PYXIS (OUSIA)

1. Pomegranate (1)
2. Narcissus Flowers (3)
3. Wheat stalks (3)
4. Cypress wood (1/2 cup pwdr.)
5. Mint (1 bundle)
6. Hellebore (1 oz)
7. Myrrh resin (1 oz)
8. Asphodel Flowers (3)
9. Garnet (1)
10. A dried bat (1)
11. Red Poppy Flowers (3)
12. Black Poppy Flowers (3)
13. Willow wood (1/2 cup pwdr.)
14. Bone from a Pig (1)
15. Black tourmaline (1)
16. Dried Cherries (1 oz)
17. Bronze Coins (3)
18. Deer antler (1 oz pwdr.)
19. Saffron (1 oz)
20. Frankincense Resin (1 oz)
21. Peridot (1)
22. Soil from a Graveyard (1 oz)
23. Soil from a flower bed (1 oz)
24. Myna bird feathers (3)

PERSEPHONE'S FESTIVALS

In the Thessalian religious calendar, two annual festivals are dedicated to honoring the divine figures of Demeter and Persephone. These important celebrations are the **Thesmophoria**, observed on October 31st, and the **Anthesteria**, held on the first dark moon of the month of Arion.[4]

THESMOPHORIA

The Thesmophoria, a cherished festival, traditionally extended over three days, with each day marked by distinct rituals. The ancient Greek celebration of Thesmophoria took place over three days.

For an extended period, scholars primarily interpreted the Thesmophoria as a fertility festival, associating the symbolic burying and exhumation of deceased pigs with the myth of Demeter and Persephone. In this ancient narrative, Persephone is abducted by Hades, destined to become his underworld consort. Demeter's profound grief for her daughter's absence causes nature to wither, and crops to wither away. Ultimately, an accord is reached among the gods, granting Persephone the opportunity to divide her time between her mother and Hades. This mythological tale serves as the origin of the changing seasons, with Persephone's presence in the underworld corresponding to winter's arrival. Scholarly analyses identified parallels between the pigs

---

[4] The religious month of Arion is from March 21st to April 19th.

interred in the pit and Persephone's stay in the underworld, while the silence observed on the second day symbolized Demeter's mourning. Furthermore, the exchange of crude and irreverent jokes during the festival was a tribute to Iambe, a servant who managed to lift Demeter's spirits during her time of profound sorrow through the use of such humor and jests.

In the realm of Thessalian religion, our approach to Thessmophoria deviates from the historical focus on agricultural aspects, instead emphasizing the mythological underpinnings. Consequently, the Thessalian Thesmophoria serves as an emotional commemoration of the *Descent of Persephone* into the Underworld and the onset of the winter months. In present times, these wintry months often cast a shadow of psychological depression and anxiety upon many people. Hence, our rituals are crafted to address and acknowledge these psychological challenges, fostering an alignment with the shifting energies. While our observance carries somber undertones, it remains infused with the hope of Persephone's impending return. Through this approach, we strive to mitigate the psychological burdens often associated with this time of year, eagerly anticipating the Young Goddess's Reawakening during the forthcoming *Anthesteria Festival* in the springtime.

THE WOMEN OF THESSALY AND THE THESMOPHORIA

The Thesmophoria also reflects the way women are seen in the Thessalian community. Thessalian women are precious, and they are revered, with a slight degree of awe. Women hold the mystical force of procreation and for this reason, they are considered semi-divine. This is why they are responsible for the Thesmophoria, to impart their semi-divine powers of procreation to the festival and promote growth and prosperity for all the people attending the holiday.

ORDER OF THE THESSALIAN THESMOPHORIA

The Thessalian festival of Thesmophoria is divided into three distinct parts.

SUNRISE – ANODOS – THE UPRISE

Early on the morning of the festival, all citizens will busy themselves preparing the festival grounds and assuring that all is ready. Foods are prepared and offerings are made to Demeter throughout the day. The opening of the day is given to a rite of union with Helios/Apollo and prayers are given to Zeus for good weather and lots of sunshine. Then the lamp or fire of Hestia is lit by carrying a flame from Her shrine to the festival grounds.

MIDDAY – NESTEIA – THE FASTING

As more celebrants arrive, each will place their offerings around the statues of Demeter and Persephone, while paying their respects to the two goddesses. Beginning at midday, it is a time of feasting and merriment. This is to celebrate the bounties of Demeter one last time before the winter months force us to conserve our food. The day is marked with various games and contests to help pass the time until nightfall. Unlike most Thessalian festivals, there is no wine or alcohol consumption during this festival, because of the somber mood soon to come, and out of respect for Demeter, who refused to drink or eat when her daughter was missing.

SUNSET – KALLIGENEIA – THE DESCENT

This is the time of Persephone's descent. The sacred objects and Persephone's statue or image (sometimes symbolized with a decorative mask) are now taken from their pedestal by the αναλυψσεια (the Revealers) and carried in a procession around the temenos. The Revealers are most commonly referred to as The Maidens and their role symbolizes the three maidens who were with Persephone, picking flowers, when she was abducted. The role of The Maidens is one of the highest honors bestowed upon Thessalian women and these ladies will undergo a seven-day purification process during which time, they must abstain from certain foods, undergo daily ritual cleansings, and are not allowed to touch or be touched by any man.

This is a procession of The Maidens is a solemn march - and all the women in attendance will wear mourning veils. The sacred objects (*these items are kept secret and known only to the citizens of Thessaly*) are then brought to the communal altar and taken out of the basket. Each person present is allowed to hold the sacred objects after first purifying their hands. The festival concludes with a solemn procession to the megara (underground vault) and Persephone's mask is placed inside and locked away until the Anthesteria.

During the period between Thesmophoria and Anthesteria, all images and statues of Demeter are covered with black cloth and hidden away from the eyes of Thessalians. This is to commemorate Demeter's retreat from the gods during Persephone's abduction.

The Maidens of Thesmophoria

FESTIVAL OF ANTHESTERIA

The Anthesteria is a sacred festival dedicated to the worship of Demeter and Persephone, the latter often referred to as Kore, symbolizing the Maiden. This celebration is intricately connected to the myth of Persephone's abduction and her subsequent return to the surface world. This myth underscores her pivotal role as the embodiment of spring's vitality and the very essence of vegetation. Just as new life emerges from the earth during spring, it recedes into the earth as the harvest season unfolds.

In its original configuration, the Anthesteria served as a jubilant festival, heralding the resurgence of Spring's vibrant spirit. This festivity extended across three days, coinciding with the Attic Calendar's month of Anthesterion, which aligns with the full moon and typically falls within January or February.

In the tapestry of Thessalian religion, the Anthesteria Festival weaves a vibrant celebration of the arrival of spring and an opportunity to pay homage to our dearly departed friends and loved ones during this season of rebirth. The Thessalian Anthesteria, a tribute to Persephone, the Queen of Hades, and Her mother Demeter, also honors the god Dionysus. It marks a time of "*first tasting*" of wine, coupled with a feast in honor of those who have passed on.

As winter's grasp loosens, the Thessalian Thesmophoria serves as a poignant reminder of Persephone's ascent from the Underworld, heralding the arrival of spring and the ensuing summer months. This is a season of jubilation, filled with light, reflection, and renewal. It is a joyous celebration, a testament to the resurgence of life on Earth, and an expression of gratitude to the gods for their boundless blessings. However, it is also a time when the gates of Hades are flung open to facilitate the Maiden's return, granting the spirits of the departed a brief period of liberty. In recognition of their presence, we set a table, laden with food and drink to satiate their hunger and thirst. As the festival concludes, we embark on a ceremonial "chase," guiding the spirits back to the gates of Hades and their rightful abode.

The name "Feast of Flowers" might imply unbridled joy, yet it also bears the weight of somber moments. When Persephone returns from the Underworld, the Gates of Hades swing ajar, allowing her to bring with her the souls of the departed, who partake in the festivities. It is a time of both reverence for our cherished departed and a gathering of the souls left unburied and untended. Some of these spirits may choose not to return to the realm of the dead when the festival concludes. Hence, the ritual's culmination encompasses a banishing ceremony, where we lovingly "chase" the spirits back to the Gates of Hades, ensuring their proper resting place.

ORDER OF THE THESSALIAN ANTHESTERIA

Much akin to the Thesmophoria, the traditional three-day Anthesteria festival has been condensed into a single day, partitioned into three distinct acts, commencing with the break of dawn.

ACT I - SUNRISE - THE PITHOIGIA

At daybreak, the festivities kick off with a sacred Dionysian ritual. An officiant, entrusted by the host or an ordained Priest or Priestess of Dionysus, blesses the wine. This blessing invokes divine protection and good spirits to safeguard the drinkers. Subsequently, libations are offered to the benevolent Agathos Daemon, Dionysus, and the Olympian deities. While attendance at this phase is entirely optional, all are welcome.

As celebrants gather, each bearing small Chythroi (terracotta pots brimming with porridge) in remembrance of the deceased, along with photographs of their beloved departed, the Altar of Hekate and Hermes takes center stage. Attendees lovingly place their cherished mementos and Chythroi at this sacred site. Afterward, they pay their respects at the Altars of Demeter and Dionysus, offering incense as a mark of devotion.

ACT II - MIDDAY - THE CHOËS

The centerpiece of the day is *Persephone's Return*, a time of profound significance. A jubilant procession to the Gates of Hades symbolizes Her resurgence. The Maidens, the same as those chosen for Thesmophoria, sing the melodious "Bring

Back the Light" as the Anthesteria Bread, crowned with a sacred mask at its heart, is carried forth, flanked by candles representing Persephone's light rekindling the world. Once the bread graces the Altar of Demeter, joyous cheers resound throughout: "Ἔχει επιστρέψει! (She has Returned!)."

In unison, attendees prepare their plates for a shared feast. Following the communal meal, they gather at the Altar of Dionysus to present offerings of incense and receive, in return, a *khus* (a large drinking vessel) brimming with wine. For the Thessalian youth reaching the age of 18, this moment signifies their rite of passage into adulthood.

The Epagoge

For Thessalian children who have reached the tender age of three during the time of the Anthesteria, a delightful ceremony known as the Epagoge marks their initiation into the religious community. In preparation, each child's parents procure a charming little wagon, lovingly adorned with vibrant blooms and colors.

The merriment commences as the children are paraded through the festival's lively grounds. Eager adults, in the spirit of a festive parade, shower the young ones with toys and gifts, adding to the enchantment of the occasion.

The grand procession culminates at the venerable Altar of Dionysus, where these budding participants receive a minuscule thimbleful of wine. This momentous sip marks their inaugural tasting of wine and holds profound significance in their Thessalian religious journey.

With this "first-tasting," they are officially inducted into the folds of the religious community, signifying the commencement of their active participation in the weekly rituals and all the forthcoming festivals. The Epagoge celebration thus warmly welcomes these youngsters into the vibrant tapestry of Thessalian religious life.

ACT III - EVENING - THE CHYTHROI

As twilight envelops the celebration, a more solemn ambiance settles in. Having reveled in the radiant return of Persephone, our beloved departed, and spiritual ancestors have joined the festivity, savoring the glow of Her presence. Yet, as darkness descends, it is time for them to return to their rightful abode in the land of the departed.

Festival leaders guide a reverent procession to the Altar of Hermes, where the Chythroi have been lovingly placed. A small quantity of flammable liquid, typically robust alcohol, is delicately poured into the Chythroi. As they ignite, the food offerings smolder for a time. At this poignant moment, everyone vocalizes the names of their beloved departed, their voices carrying their spirits to the Gates of Hades. Should young ones be in attendance, they take up the mantle to lead this rite, brandishing rattles and symbols, making joyful noise as they chase the spirits back to the gate.

EMBRACING THE SACRED RHYTHMS

Standing at the apex of our exploration into the Thessalian reverence for the esteemed goddess Persephone, it is with deep admiration and appreciation that we bring to a close this remarkable journey into the heart of an ancient and perpetually renewing tradition. Throughout our voyage, we have delved into the captivating tapestry of rituals, festivals, and customs that have forged an unbreakable bond between the Thessalian people and Persephone, the divine patroness of transition, springtime, and the realm of the Underworld, whose influence spans from the veiled mysteries to the deepest depths of human consciousness. In our steadfast endeavor to unravel the mysteries of Persephone's divine status, we have immersed ourselves in the profound traditions of Thessalian worship, where the blessings of the goddess are not merely sustenance for the body but a wellspring of spiritual connection. We have uncovered the enigmas that continue to bind the devotees of Thessaly to their sacred heritage, their mortal lives, and the goddess who graces their existence with magical insight and transformative energy. We have marveled at the enduring presence of Persephone, whose sovereignty extends from the mysterious realms to the unyielding bonds of wisdom. The Thessalian perspective on these ancient customs, as they draw parallels between the realms of mystery and the ever-evolving paths of the human spirit, imbues their observance with profound significance. From the thrill of magical pursuits to the steadfast embrace of transformative moments, we have discovered a tradition that embraces the beauty and unpredictability of life's mystical adventures. Thessalians have borne witness to the wonders of magic and have navigated the mysteries of wisdom with profound insight. In the timeless tradition of Thessalian reverence, we have not only encountered an unwavering devotion to Persephone but a way of life that recognizes the rhythms of divine inspiration and wisdom as essential components of the human journey.

As these ancient practices endure, they flourish as vibrant testimonies to the continuity of this rich tradition. As we bring this chapter to a close, we are not bidding adieu but encouraging you to embrace the ever-revolving cycles of Thessalian worship and to carry the spirit of Persephone with you on your path.

Her influence, like the mystical rites and the vast expanse of wisdom, can continue to enrich your life with the gift of resilience, the allure of wisdom, and the promise of boundless horizons. Whether you engage in mystical-centered observances during the Anthesteria, make offerings in honor of Persephone during her sacred festivals, or simply find her blessings in the enlightened pursuits of life, may you be touched by the enduring legacy of Thessalian worship and the eternal presence of Persephone herself.

As you conclude this chapter, take with you not only knowledge but the essence of magic and wisdom, and let it course through the currents of your soul as a testament to the ever-present spirit of Persephone and the timeless tradition of Thessalian reverence.

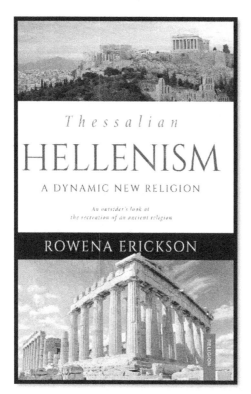

THESSALIAN HELLENISM
THE DYNAMIC NEW RELIGION

By Rowena Erickson

Established in 1994, the Church of Thessaly initially embarked on a journey to delve into the enigmatic aspects of ancient Greek religion and magical traditions. Over time, it developed its unique culture, garnering a following in the United States and Europe through its profound philosophical teachings, dynamic rituals, and religious principles. Author Rowena Erickson, a close associate of the Thessalian Tradition's founder, skillfully encapsulates the movement's essence in a succinct manner that effectively communicates its fundamental beliefs without overwhelming the reader.

ISBN: 979-8674782056

In the heart of Olympus, amidst the clash of mighty gods and the whirlwind of epic tales, there exists a goddess whose quiet strength and unwavering presence have been all too often overlooked. Hestia, the gentle guardian of the home and hearth.

The Church of Thessaly, one of the oldest Ancient Hellenic Religious organizations in the United States, presents its first book of the **Thessalian Pantheon Series**. Discover the world of ancient wisdom, warmth, and eternal fire in the captivating exploration of ancient Greek religion, mysticism and mythology.

Journey deep into the myths and mysteries that surround the goddess of home and hearth. Hestia's subtle influence is revealed, touching the lives of mortals and immortals alike. She is the unseen thread that weaves through the very fabric of existence, the embodiment of warmth in the cold, the sanctuary in the chaos, and the eternal light that guides lost souls.

MONTE PLAISANCE

MISTRESS OF EARTH AND
AGRICULTURE

DEMETER

Beneath the golden sun and among the whispers of rustling leaves, there exists a goddess whose profound influence spans the realms of nature and humanity. Meet Demeter, the Divine Mother, and embark on an extraordinary journey into the world of Greek mythology.

Church of Thessaly, one of the oldest Hellenic Religious Organizations in the United States, delves into the myths and mysteries that enshroud Demeter, the goddess of the harvest and the nurturer of life. Beyond the grand battles of the gods, her gentle strength and the eternal cycle of the seasons are unveiled, revealing a story of love, loss, and the enduring power of nature.

Discover the profound impact of this maternal deity, as she plays a pivotal role in the lives of both mortals and immortals. She is the force behind the bounty of the earth, the nurturing embrace that sustains all life, and the symbol of the ever-changing seasons.

Journey through this short book to uncover the timeless lessons of growth, resilience, and the unbreakable bonds between mother and child that Demeter represents. As you turn these pages, you will be captivated by Demeter's unwavering dedication and profound love, and you'll come to realize that her story, intertwined with the earth itself, is a reflection of the cycles of life and the enduring spirit of motherhood.

KING OF THE UNDERWORLD
HADES

In the heart of Olympus, amidst the clash of mighty gods and the whirlwind of epic tales, there exists another deity whose enigmatic presence and profound influence have been all too often overshadowed. Hades, the silent sovereign of the Underworld, emerges from the shadows in this captivating addition to the Thessalian Pantheon Series by the Church of Thessaly.

Delve deep into the enigmatic myths and mysteries that shroud Hades, the ruler of the afterlife and guardian of the souls that journey into the abyss. Beyond the thundering battles of the gods, his quiet strength and the enduring legacy of his domain are unveiled, revealing a story of duty, resilience, and the intricate balance between life and death.

Church of Thessaly invites you to explore the intricate world of Hades, the god whose realm touches the lives of both mortals and immortals. He is the keeper of the souls' destiny, the embodiment of silent authority, and the symbol of the inevitable transition from this world to the next.

This short book paints a vivid picture of Hades, the god whose presence is felt throughout the complex tapestry of Greek mythology. Journey through the ages to uncover the timeless lessons of acceptance, perseverance, and the intricate interplay between mortality and immortality.

GOD OF SEAS AND RIVERS
POSEIDON

In the heart of Thessalian religion, amidst the tumultuous waves of the Mediterranean and the majestic tales of gods and heroes, there exists a deity whose power and presence rival the boundless expanse of the sea itself—Poseidon, the God of Seas and Rivers.

Explore and unveil the myths and mysteries that enshroud Poseidon, the god of the seas, and the turbulent forces of nature. Beyond the epic battles and grand adventures, his relentless strength and unwavering command of the ocean's mysteries are unveiled, revealing a story of power, capriciousness, and the enduring connection between mankind and the sea.

Church of Thessaly, the oldest ancient Hellenic Religious Organization in the United States, invites you to explore the profound influence Poseidon exerts over the lives of both mortals and immortals. He is the master of storms, the guardian of seafarers, and the symbol of the boundless, untamed beauty, wealth, and power of the oceans.

This short book immerses you in the vast and ever-changing world of Poseidon, a deity whose presence reverberates through the waves and shores of the mortal world. Journey through the ages to uncover the timeless lessons of respect, balance, and the eternal dance between humans and the sea.

In the heart of Thessalian religion, amidst the grandeur of Olympian power and the legendary tales of gods and heroes, there is a deity whose mighty presence and dominion rival the very skies themselves—Zeus, the King of the Gods.

Journey deep into the myths and mysteries that enshroud Zeus, the god of thunder and supreme ruler of the divine realm. Beyond the epic battles and heroic quests, his unyielding might and unwavering sovereignty are unveiled, revealing a story of authority, resilience, and the enduring connection between humanity and the heavens.

The Church of Thessaly, the oldest ancient Hellenic Religious Organization in the United States, invites you to explore the profound influence Zeus exerts over both mortals and immortals. He is the master of the thunderbolt, the guardian of justice, and the symbol of celestial power and wisdom.

This short book immerses you in the expansive and ever-changing world of Zeus, a deity whose presence resounds through the skies and the hearts of mortals. Journey through the ages to uncover the timeless lessons of leadership, fairness, and the eternal relationship between humanity and the divine.

Made in the USA
Monee, IL
09 June 2024

59643891R00039